I0489001

Legal Notice

Disclaimer Notice

The Ultimate Guide To Leadership:

Leadership Development Key

Develop Self Confidence, Become A Great Leader, And Unlock Your Limitless Potential!

Ryan Cooper

STOP!!! Before you read any further....Would you like to know the Secrets of Transforming your life, overcome insecurities, develop leadership skills, and undeniable confidence in your personal, professional, and relationship life?

If your answer is yes, then you are not alone. Thousands of people are looking for the secret to have unstoppable confidence and self-driven power in all areas of their lives.

If you have been searching for these answers without much luck, you're in the right place!

Not only will you gain incredible insight in this book, but because I want to make sure to give you as much value as possible, right now for a limited time you can get full **100% FREE access to a VIP bonus EBook** entitled **LIMITLESS ENERGY!**

<u>**Just Go Here For Free Instant Access:**</u>

<u>**www.PotentialRise.com**</u>

Table Of Contents

Introduction

I want to thank you and congratulate you for purchasing the book, *"Leadership Development Key: The Ultimate Guide To Leadership! Develop Self Confidence, Become A Great Leader, And Unlock Your Limitless Potential!"*.

One of the most essential questions mankind has always wondered about is what makes an effective leader? Why is that some people's presence alone demands that they be followed, while others seem to have difficulty making their dog follow them!

This book focuses on how you might develop the essential qualities of a leader. By saying "unlock," we ought to define that leadership is, the different kinds of leaders, the implications of the different types of leadership, and the development of desired leadership qualities.

Often, leaders are not recognized until they eventually leave us. While great leaders are known to inspire employees and to initiate singular movement in organizations, their impact in our lives remains underappreciated until they go away. But do you need to actually leave your present company in order for your contributions to be "officially" recognized? More importantly, do we, as employees, need to see someone go before we see him as a leader?

We've known great people, and we've seen some of them pass on. Jobs, Mandela, Lincoln, and even Mao Zedong, are venerated as leaders in their own right. We have Lee Kwan Yu, Bill Gates, Jeff Bezos, Larry Page, and Kwon Oh Hyun as present – day individuals who are pushing organizational and political leadership to new heights. Do we need to be like them in order to be recognized as leaders?

We can all go on asking questions about leadership, but one fact remains: we are all endowed with the potential to lead. Because of that, we also have the potential to become great leaders. If you wallowed in such thought for a long time now, don't you think it's about time that you step up and rule the world?

This book will help you unlock your potential. Sit back, and enjoy the ride.

Chapter 1:.Unlocking The Leadership DNA

What do leaders have in common? If you make a list of all business leaders and list all of their traits, you'll only be able to answer this question by establishing their commonalities. A better way to answer this question then is to analyze the qualities of effective leaders using an objective standpoint. Let's go through the different strands that make effective leaders.

Leaders see the future

Leaders are visionaries. They have an ongoing hunger for knowledge that is marked by intense curiosity. As a result, they have their own unique vision of a company's future, and work real hard to make it happen as soon as they assume their seat. Because their point of view is unique, leaders are responsible for one major hallmark of effective leadership: coherent movement.

Coherent movement is marked by singularity such that one hand knows what the other is doing. And because everyone is moving in the same direction, the future, as envisioned by the leader, is within reach.

Leaders see results

Leaders always look for results. Leaders always deliver results. And leaders always make sure that results happen. An organization has to keep moving. If it's new, it has to reach a milestone. If it's been there for decades, it has to sustain its momentum. Lose the momentum, and you might lose it all. With the density of competition out there right now, leaders are always on their feet because they'll never know if their competitor is out to get them – for good reason.

And when it comes to result, leaders ensure that targets are delivered. After all, what's a goal for if it's not to be achieved? This brings about one characteristic an effective leader has: decision – making.

Leaders communicate

This is true to some organizations now: some leaders no longer have time to reach out to the frontlines and see how things are going for them. Communication is powerful enough that it can move mountains. When a leader goes down and talks to those people who are doing the "dirty work," they make things look fine even when it's not. The soothing effect they have on employees is immeasurable. Plus, they get a chance to reignite one's passion for the organization.

By being able to communicate, effective leaders bring about one important factor in human resource development: strengthening others. If a leader can empower his people, his people will empower him further. The give and take relationship cannot be denied. At this point, a popular leader may not be a good communicator. If that's the case, is he effective?

Leaders develop

Leaders don't only eye the evolution of their organization. They also eye the development of their people. If people continuously see growth in their careers, they become more motivated to work. Because they are motivated to work, organizational goals are met, and the company advances to the next milestone.

This quality breeds one characteristic of effective leadership: building relationships. If leaders seek to develop their manpower, they'll be able to build relationships that help the company grow. If such relationship grows deeper, it breeds passion.

Leaders walk their talk

Traditional leaders have been seen a commanders – people whose primary task is to bark orders to their subordinates. Not now; that has changed. Presently, leaders are considered followers. A leader doesn't usually get the respect he needs if he does not practice what he preaches.

If a leader is able to walk his talk, he becomes charismatic. Charisma is what makes the organization mobile. Afterwards, we're back to square one: movement towards a goal as a single entity, with passion, and with positive relationships.

The qualities of an effective leader seem to be too theoretical above. To date, no one has come forward claiming that he has all of the finest qualities that a leader should have. That's because all of these traits are developed. They are acquired and are not endowed as a natural gift. While people are born persuasive, they have their attitude to work on. And since no one is perfect, we all start from scratch.

In the next chapter, let's meet the different types of leaders and scrutinize their impact in today's organizations.

Chapter 2:.The Types Of Leaders

The classification of leaders found in this chapter has been there since the concept of leadership has been established. Let's go through them anyway before we discuss what you can do to develop your leadership potential.

The Laissez-Faire Leader

There are leaders who are not fond of supervising their employees. While this type of leadership is useful in organizations where employees are highly trained and are highly experienced, it is not possible to find an organization with zero learners. They say that we always learn something new at work, and that proves true. So what if there are employees that needs supervision?

The implications of this type of leadership are clear: poor production, poor efficiency, and increased costs.

People who believe in this type of leadership usually present two arguments. First, is that employees are responsible for their own learning. Second, employees should be responsible and accountable for their own actions.

However, if there's no one to teach them, how can they learn? And how will they even know what they need to learn? If they're also accountable and responsible for their actions, who will they know if they're going beyond their limits?

The Autocratic Leader

There are leaders who do make it a point to impose their decisions without consulting managers or employees. To challenge them is a crime and to evaluate the merits of their decision is a capital offense. As a result, this type of leader is highly involved in the different functions of his organization, but not so much on his employees.

The implications of this leadership type are as follows: feelings of powerlessness among employees, limited development potential for talented employees, and resistance towards the decision – maker.

There are people who believe in this type of leadership. They say that being autocratic helps solidify the organization so it acts with coherence. They also believe that amidst the differences people in the organization have; it pays to balance things out by confining authority for decision – making to a single body of people or a person.

However, if employees feel empowered, it would appear as though they're acting against their will. There will be no freedom, and they will lax over matters that need decision. The impact: delayed productivity until decision arrives.

The Participative Leader

Also referred to as the Democratic Leader, the Participative Leader involves employees in the decision – making process. This type of leadership causes employee morale to boost because employees are able to make their own contributions before decisions are implemented.

The implication of this leadership style is seen in the work environment. Productivity is increased, efficiency is also increased, and employees will feel generally happy in the workplace.

However, while Participative Leadership seems to be more accommodating in nature, it also has its own potential drawbacks. Ideally, the final decision will come from the leader as a result of evaluating the different opinions of employees. If the leader does not enforce that idea, employee willpower might overwhelm him causing organizational paralysis.

The Transactional Leader

This type of leadership is based on the reward and punishment model. The operational word here is "consequence." What happens is a leader meets with employees to agree or organizational goals. Since goals are predetermined, a "contract" is established between the leader and the employees about agreement to pre-set goals.

The result of this type of leadership is goal accomplishment. In effect, a leader is given the right to review and evaluate employee performance and reserves the right to impose sanctions or rewards based on the result.

While this type of leadership works well in a results-driven environment, there's a catch: if the "punishment" is punitive, it might cause fear among employees about not being able to meet a goal. Note that fear is a de-motivator which connotes negative results.

The Transformational Leader

This type of leadership involves a high degree of communication and visibility. Organizations with leaders of this type will see their managers and executives immerse themselves in the daily operations of the company. The transformative element under this style is demonstrated by constantly talking to employees about enhancing current performance.

The implication of this type of leadership is clear: if leaders are involved in reaching for company goals, employees tend to work better because the management is also working with them.

As far as pitfalls are concerned, transformational leaders, when not careful, may smother employees. Because they mingle with employees in the workplace, leaders also have to be tolerant and understanding of the different characteristics of the people they deal with. If leaders are not that sociable, they might not be able to realize the benefits of this leadership style.

So by refreshing your memory about the different leadership styles above, what can you deduce? Observe the current leaders in your own organization, and notice how they seem to embrace all of the styles given above. Understandably, leadership styles depend on context. There are times when being autocratic is best, there are times when involving employees is better, and so on. The remaining question then is, *what do you need to become a leader*? The answer is in the next chapter.

Chapter 3: What You Need To Become A Leader

Without much ado, the answer to the question in the previous chapter is this: learning. It is said that leadership is an acquired trait. Some are born with a seemingly fluent skill in persuasion, but the rest of the leadership skills are learned in action. So what steps can you take? And what is it exactly that you're supposed to learn?

Learn how to communicate effectively

Communication is important in every setting that we involve ourselves in. At work, communication is something that bridges the gap between performance and goal attainment, so avoid these pitfalls: talking down on people lest they'll feel belittled, asking close-ended questions lest they won't get creative using excessive authority lest they'll grow fearful, and promoting a culture of unanimity lest they'll become dependent.

In contrast, you'll be able to communicate more effectively when you exercise active listening to put value on every individual's idea, when you display gratitude for their openness and their contributions, when you provide constructive feedback to recognize the different aspects of their performance, when you don't focus too much on your authority and treat employees as your partners, and when you avoid that black and white attitude of "I'm right; you're wrong."

Learn how to be everybody's friend

Displaying enthusiasm at work is contagious, and people expect that the source of such is their leader. But merely showing off an excited demeanor is not enough. In fact, there are leaders who are aloof to the point of avoiding employee interaction, who are intolerant to the point of not allowing mistakes to happen, who are unfair to the point of limiting growth opportunities for some people, and who are selfish to the point of putting their gains before everyone else's.

To get past the risk of spurning avoidance in the workplace, be friendly by respecting each of your employees and by acknowledging their ideas, be understanding by acknowledging that everyone makes mistakes and that there's room for improvement, be fair by providing equal opportunities for sharing and growth for all of your employees, and be a person of integrity by tying your goals with the goals of your employees.

Learn to inspire everyone

It seems hard to inspire everyone to work towards a common goal. However, that's only on a perception basis. This means that if you think that you group won't be able to hit the goal; you'll be prone to displaying behaviors that will not motivate them. So avoid these pitfalls: don't be too narrow when it comes to goal discussions, don't be too strict about hitting the goal and nothing else, don't be too biased to the point of stifling the group to pursue your goals, and don't be too distant to discourage open communication.

Instead of being a source of de-motivation, become the beacon of inspiration by becoming the ultimate support that your group needs, by becoming the guide that they need when it comes to reorienting them towards your goals, by becoming a source of encouragement by appreciating employee milestones and extra efforts, by becoming mediator when it comes to group disagreements over goal attainment, and by becoming a participative member in discussions, and by considering everyone else's opinions.

Learn who your people are

This is not something literal, and it gets quite a difficult thing to do if you're leading a group of a hundred individuals. But don't let that stop you. Don't be the kind of leader who refuses to interact with different employees in different levels, don't be the kind of leader who doesn't even recognize his employees, and will only do so if you see their IDs, and don't be the kind of leader who stays on his desk all day – totally absent in the view of employees.

To learn who your people are, be a leader who interacts with everyone. There mere gesture of greeting people in the elevator proves to be effective in keeping members motivated. If possible, seek to remember the names of the people in your organization even if you can only go as far as your middle managers. In effect, get to know each of your member's skills, qualities, and characteristics. As an offshoot of your doing so here, you'll be able to learn the next one on our list.

Learn how to treat others as individuals

There are leaders who consider their people are a means to an end. They're using other people to accomplish the things they themselves cannot do. And because that's the case, their workplace is expected to be characterized by people-orientedness. Sadly, it's not the case for leaders who disregard each person's expectations from the company, who discourages creative expression of ideas and work methods, who withdraw rewards (even through compliments), and who refuse to delegate because of lack of trust.

By acting the opposite, you'll learn how to value each individual within your team or your organization. How? Start by acknowledging that each person in the company or the team has a set of expectations in the same way as you have your expectations from them. Be creative as you introduce new ways in job performance to ease the boredom caused by repetitive work. Introduce incentives in order to recognize each individual's contribution to the team or organization. And finally, learn to delegate trust in order to make each group member proud of having contributed to the team or the organization's accomplishments.

Learn how to get things done

Some leaders think that because they have subordinates working for them, they can sit around and wait for work to be done. While delegation of work is a part of an organization, an effective leader is someone who does not sit around and wait, who withholds information and is selfish on knowledge and skills-sharing, who is proud enough to seek for advice, who is indecisive, and who particularly turns down tasks that are out of this scope.

In order to become a good leader, you should learn how to: take initiative by becoming a model in assuming tasks that are yet to be completed, share your knowledge and skills in order to help people who have difficulties, ask for advice in order to foster goal accomplishment and involvement among your team members, be decisive, enthusiastic, and energetic in order to help get things done, and saying "no" in a polite manner when you already have enough tasks in your hands.

Learn how to solve problems methodically

Being methodical means utilizing a step-by-step approach to problem-solving. This part is where all of the six concepts discussed above are tested as you show your team or your organization your approach towards challenging times. It will also help you demonstrate your ability to arrive at effective decisions that solves the problem, helps your team, and tides your organization through in order to move forward. So what should you learn?

First, you need to identify the problem in the simplest and clearest manner possible. Second, you need to gather enough information about the problem. Third, you need to explore solutions. Fourth, you need to evaluate solutions. Fifth, you need to plan for the implementation of that solution, and sixth, you need to do follow-up in order to measure the effectiveness of that solution.

Take note that the methods enumerated above may or may not involve your team or your employees. However, in light of shared responsibility over the company, and in light with the knowledge possessed by your employees (some of which you may not know), getting them involved makes problem-solving a collaborative effort.

The points for learning above are all beautiful, and only one thing will stop you from learning them: self-perception. Do you think of yourself as a capable leader? Why or why not? Do you want to be a leader? Then let's see how you can change the way you look at your self in the next chapter.

Chapter 4: Self-Perception And Great Leadership

Self-knowledge – a term that succinctly capture the definition of self-perception. Since it implies knowledge of the self, it involves the set of negative and positive attributes. In the context of leadership, assessing yourself as someone capable of leading is as important as your methods in leadership. If, at this time, you're experiencing self-doubt, these tips will help you see the bright side in becoming a leader with limitless potential.

It's all in your head

Henry Ford said, "Whether you think you can, or you think you can't--you're right." No one can dispel your self-misconceptions except you. Realize that in order to start becoming a leader, you need a healthy mindset, and a component of a healthy mindset believes that you can be a great leader.

It's not in others

It is true that we tend to follow the best practices that great leaders have. Great leaders are the people we respect, and not necessarily those who are rich and famous. But that doesn't mean embracing all of their key attributes. It also means cultivating a unique character as you practice becoming a leader. This unique character will set you apart.

It's not about comparison

If you don't believe in your ability as a leader, and if you keep on comparing yourself to others, you'll end up focusing on the attributes that you lack. Know that you can't have it all. Instead of feeling insecure about what don't have, feel secured by the things that you have. These attributes will help you move your way to the top.

It's in your inner speech

What you tell yourself becomes your reality. So if you tell yourself you can't do it, you probably can't - forever. If you inhibit your leadership potential by defeating yourself with self-defeating thoughts, you'll never realize your potentials. So love yourself. Love it so much that you encourage yourself to become the kind of leader you're meant to be.

It's in the future

This is where the successful people differ from the unsuccessful ones: imagination. We're all given the power to imagine great things, but some of us only get that far and stay there forever. Others go on and on until they become champions in their own field. Take your pick: will you perceive yourself as a stuck-up person in the future, or will you see yourself as someone who inspires people to go on?

It's in your efforts

Yes, you're not perfect. And no one is. For all you know, someone you're envious of may also be envious of you. There's such a thing as compensation – it's a concept in Psychology that deals with how people fill in their lacking by pursuing activities that capitalizes on their strengths. The result is remarkable: people who compensate will end up loving themselves not only for their achievements, but also for their underachievement.

There's no step-by-step approach towards improving your self-perception. If you've hear someone say that you are responsible for your own learning, this is where you can use that. Begin by changing your mindset and everything else will follow. In the end, you'll get to where you want to be. If you're in a leadership role now, but are still trying to figure out how you can be better, evaluating your perceptions about yourself and your leadership is a good way to start. James Allen, the author of the popular book *As a Man Thinketh*, said, "You are today where your thoughts have brought you; you will be tomorrow where your thoughts take you."

Conclusion

Thank you again for purchasing this book on how to unlock your limitless potential as a great leader!

I am extremely excited to pass this information along to you, and I am so happy that you now have read and can hopefully implement these strategies going forward.

I hope this book was able to help you understand what it will take for you to become the leader you wish to be.

The next step is to get started using this information and to begin reaping the benefits of your new found leadership.

If you know of anyone else that could benefit from the information presented here please inform them of this book.

Finally, if you enjoyed this book and feel it has added value to your life in any way, please take the time to share your thoughts and post a review on Amazon. It'd be greatly appreciated!

Thank you and good luck!

Preview Of:

<u>Visualization Techniques</u>

Creative Visualization Techniques And Visualization Meditation Guide To Achieve Goals And Optimal Mindset Success!

Introduction

I want to thank you and congratulate you for purchasing the book, *Visualization Techniques - Creative Visualization Techniques And Visualization Meditation Guide To Achieve Goals And Optimal Mindset Success!*

This book contains insight on how you can design your life through proper visualization in regards to your individual life blueprint.

Do you know what you want most in life? If so, you are on the right track! Now you need to learn the proper way to draw a blueprint for your plan on paper and most importantly, in your mind.

If you want to build a hotel, a golf course, a car, or simply a house, you would need one thing - a vision of what you want to build, and a plan to build it.

Reaching for your goals is much the same. Just as you would need a great architect to build a fine building, you need to be the architect of your own life. You need to be armed with the understanding of how to visualize what you want, and also to understand how to obtain plans for your endeavor. This book will serve as a reference to mind architecture and how you can use it.

Thanks again for purchasing this book. I hope you enjoy it!

Chapter 1: Visualization - How Can It Help You Succeed

Visualization is creating images in your mind of you doing or having something that you want, and repeating them over and over again. It is a mental trick that allows you to feel and live the images you create in your brain as if they are actually happening. For example, you can imagine yourself being the successful person that you want, heal the illness that has been bothering you for a while, being able to close an important deal or having a great relationship. You can do your visualization every day for five minutes.

Visualization is not about hoping that someday, what you aspire will happen or that it will build your confidence so that you can fulfill your goals someday. You visualize in your mind that you already have what you want and you are already living the life that you have always dreamt of. Although you are aware at one level that visualization is a mental trick, your subconscious cannot distinguish between imagination and reality. It acts upon the images that you create within your mind. It doesn't matter if these images are the reflection of your current reality or not.

To achieve your goal, visualization can help by:

- Allowing you to become consciously aware of the things that can help you achieve your desired outcome by visualizing it over and over again in your mind. Visualization helps you get rid of anything that does not correspond to the image that you are visualizing.

Continuously visualizing your desired outcome in your mind involves all the cells in your body to that image and you mirror and reverberate with everything that goes in harmony with that frequency, both in the physical and non-physical level. This frequency lets you move towards everything that you need in order to manifest your desired image.

- Letting you impress your desired idea to your subconscious mind which eventually becomes fixed so that your body automatically moves toward and attract whatever you desire. Athletes use visualization because they are conditioning their mind so that their bodies will act the way they wanted them to without exerting much effort. Visualization allows a person to become unconsciously competent wherein competence becomes a natural part of your being. This idea works the same with successful people. These people repeats their desired outcome in their minds over and over again until their bodies automatically does whatever is needed to turn their dreams into a physical reality.

The mind is very powerful. It is the tool that helps you understand the world that you live in. Through visualization, you are able to experience your dreams even before it becomes a physical reality. It allows you to get a taste of your desired outcome which helps stimulate your burning desire to turn it into a reality. Focusing intently on something that you desire for yourself allows you to feel the emotions that you would feel in the actual event, allowing you to live the moment before it becomes a reality.

When you stay true to yourself and you visualize the best future for you, this future will spark a burning desire within you and if you properly feed it, will continually burn until your dreams become a reality. Visualizing your desired future over and over again will make you want it so dearly that you will do everything to turn it into reality.

Visualization allows you to focus on your desired future and helps you determine the things that can help you to turn this dream into a reality. Visualization moves you towards your dream wherein you automatically do what is necessary to manifest your dream into a physical reality.

Thanks for Previewing My Exciting Book Entitled:

"Visualization Techniques: Creative Visualization Techniques And Visualization Meditation Guide To Achieve Goals And Optimal Mindset Success!

To purchase this book, simply go to the Amazon Kindle store and simply search:

"VISUALIZATION TECHNIQUES"

Then just scroll down until you see my book. You will know it is mine because you will see my name "Ryan Cooper" underneath the title.

Alternatively, you can visit my author page on Amazon to see this book and other work I have done. Thanks so much, and please don't forget your free bonuses

DON'T LEAVE YET! - YOUR FREE BONUSES ARE BELOW!

Free Bonus Offer: Get Free Access To The PotentialRise.com VIP Newsletter!

Once you enter your email address you will immediately get free access to this awesome newsletter!

But wait, right now if you join now for free you will also get free access to the "LIMITLESS ENERGY" free EBook!

To claim both your FREE VIP NEWSLETTER MEMBERSHIP and your FREE BONUS Ebook on LIMITLESS ENERGY!

Just Go To:

www.PotentialRise.com